A Guide to Being a Christian Gentleman

Dedicated to my son Joseph

Since the time you were born I realized you are extraordinary. I entrusted you in God's hands and He has shaped you into a great young man. I look forward to your growth in the Lord and in life. ~ Mom

Printed in the United States of America
First Printing, 2021

ISBN: 978-0-9987952-9-4

Cover Design: Sheena Crawford
Publisher: Sheena Crawford

This gift is for _____

I pray it blesses you.

From _____

Date _____

Contents

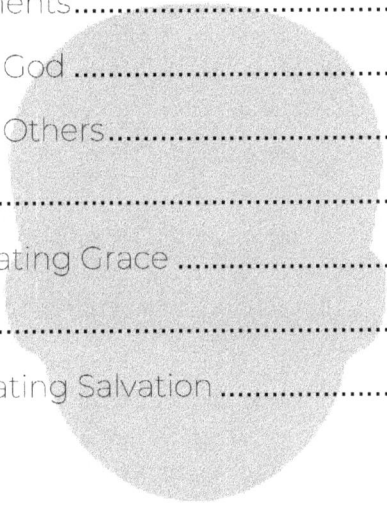

Financial

#1 – Planning Finances

Be planful with your future and finances.

The plans of the diligent lead surely to plenty, but those of everyone who is hasty, surely to poverty. ~ Proverbs 21:5

#2 – Taking Action on Plans

Take action on your plans, not just talking about them.

In all labor there is profit, but idle chatter leads only to poverty. ~ Proverbs 14:23

#3 – Being a Good Steward

Be a good steward over money ensuring it's not wasted or squandered.

He who is faithful in what is least is faithful also in much; and he who is unjust in what is least is unjust also in much.
~ Luke 16:10

#4 – Planning Inheritance

Have inheritance for your children (savings, life insurance, etc.)

A good man leaves an inheritance to his children's children, but the wealth of the sinner is stored up for the righteous. ~ Proverbs 13:22

#5 – Avoiding Debt

Practice discipline by temporarily making financial cuts and saving to buy what you want, without debt.

Owe no man any thing, but to love one another: for he that loveth another hath fulfilled the law. ~ Romans 13:8

#6 – Being Modest

Be modest in your apparel and purchases and feel no need to prove your value to anyone else.

For the love of money is a root of all kinds of evil, for which some have strayed from the faith in their greediness, and pierced themselves through with many sorrows. ~ 1 Timothy 6:10

#7 – Caring for Possessions

Take care of your possessions including home, car, clothes, and shoes.

Moreover it is required in stewards that one be found faithful. ~ 1 Corinthians 4:2

#8 – Helping Those in Need

Have a caring and generous heart for those in need.

But whoever has this world's goods, and sees his brother in need, and shuts up his heart from him, how does the love of God abide in him? My little children, let us not love in word or in tongue, but in deed and in truth. ~ 1 John 3:17-18

Physical

#9 – Having Proper Hygiene

Have proper hygiene by brushing hair and teeth and staying clean.

And when he who has a discharge is cleansed of his discharge, then he shall count for himself seven days for his cleansing, wash his clothes, and bathe his body in running water; then he shall be clean. ~ Leviticus 15:13

#10 – Dressing Respectably

Dress properly and in a respectable manner.

Or do you not know that your body is the temple of the Holy Spirit who is in you, whom you have from God, and you are not your own? For you were bought at a price; therefore glorify God in your body and in your spirit, which are God's. ~ 1 Corinthians 6:19-20

#11 – Taking Care of Body

Take care of your body by eating healthy and exercising so you can properly take care of others.

Beloved, I pray that you may prosper in all things and be in health, just as your soul prospers. ~ 3 John 2

#12 – Marking Your Body

Keep your body free from markings and tattoos.

You shall not make any cuttings in your flesh for the dead, nor tattoo any marks on you: I am the Lord. ~ Leviticus 19:28

Mental

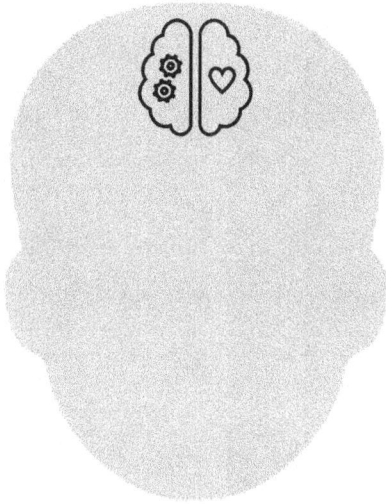

#13 – Learning and Growing

Be humble and continue learning and growing either formally or informally.

And do not be conformed to this world, but be transformed by the renewing of your mind, that you may prove what is that good and acceptable and perfect will of God. ~ Romans 12:2

#14 – Sharing Emotions

Be emotionally intelligent and able to communicate emotions maturely.

A wrathful man stirs up strife, but he who is slow to anger allays contention. ~ Proverbs 15:18

#15 – Showing Sad Emotions

It's okay to cry and show healthy emotions.

A time to weep, and a time to laugh; a time to mourn, and a time to dance. ~ Ecclesiastes 3:4

#16 – Making Decisions

Make wise decisions and seek God's counsel and the counsel of godly men.

Listen to counsel and receive instruction, that you may be wise in your latter days. There are many plans in a man's heart, nevertheless the Lord's counsel - that will stand. ~ Proverbs 19:20-21

#17 – Enjoying the Present

Enjoy the present moments.

Come now, you who say, "Today or tomorrow we will go to such and such a city, spend a year there, buy and sell, and make a profit"; whereas you do not know what will happen tomorrow. For what is your life? It is even a vapor that appears for a little time and then vanishes away. ~ James 4:13-14

#18 – Responding to Stress

Pray to God if you ever feel distressed.

As for me, I will call upon God, and the Lord shall save me. Evening and morning and at noon I will pray, and cry aloud, and He shall hear my voice. ~ Psalm 55:16-17

#19 – Asking for Help

Discern when to ask for help and delegate.

Both you and these people who are with you will surely wear yourselves out. For this thing is too much for you; you are not able to perform it by yourself. ~ Exodus 18:18

#20 – Trusting in God

Learn to trust God, He is always faithful and constant.

Commit your way to the Lord, trust also in Him, and He shall bring it to pass. ~ Psalm 37:5

Family

#21 – Honoring Parents

Show value toward your father and mother, despite the circumstances of your childhood.

Honor your father and your mother, that your days may be long upon the land which the Lord your God is giving you. ~ Exodus 20:12

#22 – Addressing Women

Call ladies by their name, with another respectable title, or Miss or Ma'am if you do not know their name.

Older women as mothers, younger women as sisters, with all purity. ~ 1 Timothy 5:2

#23 – Choosing a Wife

Choose a wife that consistently exemplifies the characteristics of God.

Do not be unequally yoked together with unbelievers. For what fellowship has righteousness with lawlessness? And what communion has light with darkness? ~ 2 Corinthians 6:14

#24 – Caring for Your Wife

Care for the wellbeing of your wife.

(e.g. Clean your lady's car off if there is snow. Clean the driveway or other driving areas that could be hazardous. Walk closest to the curb when you're with your lady to ensure she's shielded.)

Who can find a virtuous wife? For her worth is far above rubies. The heart of her husband safely trusts her; so he will have no lack of gain. ~ Proverbs 31:10-11

#25 – Valuing Your Wife

Show your wife that she is valued.

(e.g. Offer your coat, jacket, or umbrella if your lady is cold or getting wet. Open doors or pull out chairs for your lady.)

Husbands, love your wives, just as Christ also loved the church and gave Himself for her. ~ Ephesians 5:25

#26 – Caring for Family

Care for the wellbeing of your family.

But if anyone does not provide for his own, and especially for those of his household, he has denied the faith and is worse than an unbeliever. ~ 1 Timothy 5:8

#27 – Teaching Children

Teach your children how to be respectable young gentlemen and ladies.

You shall teach them diligently to your children, and shall talk of them when you sit in your house, when you walk by the way, when you lie down, and when you rise up. ~ Deuteronomy 6:7

Relational

#28 – Sharing Your Thoughts

Share your point of view after listening and gathering information needed to be informed.

So then, my beloved brethren, let every man be swift to hear, slow to speak, slow to wrath. ~ James 1:19

#29 – Dismissing Arguments

Walk away from arguments with men that are clearly fruitless and pointless.

It is honorable for a man to stop striving, since any fool can start a quarrel. ~ Proverbs 20:3

#30 – Forgiving Others

Forgive people that hurt you.

For if you forgive men their trespasses, your heavenly Father will also forgive you. ~ Matthew 6:14

#31 – Setting Boundaries

Set appropriate boundaries and expectations with people in your life to guard your heart.

Keep your heart with all diligence, for out of it spring the issues of life. ~ Proverbs 4:23

#32 – Being Positive

Smile and laugh often, it brightens yours and other people's day.

A merry heart does good, like medicine, but a broken spirit dries the bones. ~ Proverbs 17:22

#33 – Prioritizing Peace

Be quick to move toward peace and defend yourself with the power and grace of God if necessary.

Pursue peace with all people, and holiness, without which no one will see the Lord. ~ Hebrews 12:14

#34 – Showing Care

Show care and gentleness toward the poor, elderly, women, and children.

And let us not grow weary while doing good, for in due season we shall reap if we do not lose heart. Therefore, as we have opportunity, let us do good to all, especially to those who are of the household of faith. ~ Galatians 6:9-10

#35 – Ensuring Safety

Wait until your family or friends are safely inside the house before driving away.

Let each of you look out not only for his own interests, but also for the interests of others.
~ Philippians 2:4

#36 – Encouraging Others

Lift others up by encouraging them and being a light.

You are the light of the world. A city that is set on a hill cannot be hidden. Let your light so shine before men, that they may see your good works and glorify your Father in heaven. ~ Matthew 5:14,16

#37 – Choosing Words Wisely

Consider what you're about to say, before you say it.

Walk in wisdom toward those who are outside, redeeming the time. Let your speech always be with grace, seasoned with salt, that you may know how you ought to answer each one. ~ Colossians 4:5-6

#38 – Leading Others

Lead with a mindset and purpose of serving the needs of others.

Yet it shall not be so among you; but whoever desires to become great among you, let him be your servant. ~ Matthew 20:26

Character

#39 – Keeping Your Word

Keep your word. If you're unsure if your word can be kept, communicate that expectation clearly.

But whoever keeps His word, truly the love of God [a]is perfected in him. By this we know that we are in Him. ~ 1 John 2:5

#40 – Being On Time

Be on time or a few minutes early to appointments, work, and when invited to events.

He who has a slack hand becomes poor, but the hand of the diligent makes rich. ~ Proverbs 10:4

#41 – Being Strong

Have strength and courage to follow through in everything you set your mind to do.

Be strong and of good courage, do not fear nor be afraid of them; for the Lord your God, He is the One who goes with you. He will not leave you nor forsake you. ~ Deuteronomy 31:6

#42 – Having Confidence

Let your honesty, integrity, and trustworthiness show your confidence.

In all things showing yourself to be a pattern of good works; in doctrine showing integrity, reverence, incorruptibility, sound speech that cannot be condemned, that one who is an opponent may be ashamed, having nothing evil to say of you. ~ Titus 2:7-8

#43 – Being Grateful

Be grateful and thank God for your blessings.

In everything give thanks; for this is the will of God in Christ Jesus for you. ~ 1 Thessalonians 5:18

#44 – Improving Self

An apology should be followed by a change in behavior.

Afterward Jesus found him in the temple, and said to him, "See, you have been made well. Sin no more, lest a worse thing come upon you." ~ John 5:14

#45 – Doing What's Right

Do what is right according to God's Word.

Therefore, to him who knows to do good and does not do it, to him it is sin. ~ James 4:17

#46 – Being Decisive

Confirm decisions with God and be decisive.

But let him ask in faith, with no doubting, for he who doubts is like a wave of the sea driven and tossed by the wind. ~ James 1:6

Spiritual

#47 – Putting God First

Put God first in everything you do.

You shall love the Lord your God with all your heart, with all your soul, and with all your strength. ~ Deuteronomy 6:5

#48 – Following God

Allow God to guide you.

However, when He, the Spirit of truth, has come, He will guide you into all truth; for He will not speak on His own authority, but whatever He hears He will speak; and He will tell you things to come. ~ John 16:13

#49 - Praying

Pray for yourself and your family daily.

If you abide in Me, and My words abide in you, you[a] will ask what you desire, and it shall be done for you. ~ John 15:7

#50 - Fasting

Fast for yourself and your family.

Is this not the fast that I have chosen: to loose the bonds of wickedness, to undo the heavy burdens, to let the oppressed go free, and that you break every yoke? ~ Isaiah 58:6

#51 – Staying Consistent

Stay consistent with your morals and values.

And if it seems evil to you to serve the Lord, choose for yourselves this day whom you will serve, whether the gods which your fathers served that were on the other side of the River, or the gods of the Amorites, in whose land you dwell. But as for me and my house, we will serve the Lord. ~ Joshua 24:15

Commandments

Commandments are anything God tells us to do and a common example is when God commanded Joshua to be strong and have good courage in Joshua 1:9. There are also ten formal commandments (Exodus 20) that are expected to be kept. God's commandments are the highest of His law.

#52 – Loving God

Jesus said to him, 'You shall love the Lord your God with all your heart, with all your soul, and with all your mind.'
~ Matthew 22:37

1. You shall have no other gods before Me.

2. You shall not make for yourself a carved image—any likeness *of anything* that *is* in heaven above, or that *is* in the

earth beneath, or that *is* in the water under the earth; you shall not bow down to them nor serve them. For I, the Lord your God, *am* a jealous God, visiting the iniquity of the fathers upon the children to the third and fourth *generations* of those who hate Me, but showing mercy to thousands, to those who love Me and keep My commandments.

3. You shall not take the name of the Lord your God in vain, for the Lord will not hold him guiltless who takes His name in vain.

4. Remember the Sabbath day, to keep it holy. Six days you shall labor and do all your work, but the seventh day *is* the Sabbath of the Lord your God. *In it* you shall do no work: you, nor your son, nor your daughter, nor your male servant, nor your female

servant, nor your cattle, nor your stranger who *is* within your gates. For *in* six days the Lord made the heavens and the earth, the sea, and all that *is* in them, and rested the seventh day. Therefore the Lord blessed the Sabbath day and hallowed it.

#53 – Loving Others

You shall love your neighbor as yourself. ~ Matthew 22:39

5. Honor your father and your mother, that your days may be long upon the land which the Lord your God is giving you.

6. You shall not kill.

7. You shall not commit adultery.

8. You shall not steal.

9. You shall not bear false witness against your neighbor.

10. You shall not covet your neighbor's house; you shall not covet your neighbor's wife, nor his male servant, nor his female servant, nor his ox, nor his donkey, nor anything that *is* your neighbor's.

Statutes

Statutes are holy requirements instituted by God. This includes Holy Days like the Day of Atonement and the Feast of Tabernacles (Leviticus 23). God specifically said that many of the statutes should be kept "forever" and God does not contradict Himself. If there ever appears to be a contradiction, it is in our understanding, not in the Word of God. To be clear,

Yeshua is our offering and sacrifice so we're no longer expected to make animal offerings or sacrifices on the Holy Days. The Holy Days that are statutes are expected to be honored though (not man-made "Holi-Days").

#54 – Celebrating Grace

Beware lest anyone cheat you through philosophy and empty deceit, according to the tradition of men, according to the basic principles of the world, and not according to Christ. ~ Colossians 2:8

If they break My statutes and do not keep My commandments, then I will punish their transgression with the rod,

and their iniquity with stripes.
Nevertheless My
lovingkindness I will not utterly
take from him,
nor allow My faithfulness to fail.
~ Psalm 89:31-33

Therefore be imitators of God
as dear children. And walk in
love, as Christ also has loved us
and given Himself for us, an
offering and a sacrifice to God
for a sweet-smelling aroma. ~
Ephesians 5:1-2

Also the tenth *day* of this seventh month *shall be* the Day of Atonement. It shall be a holy convocation for you; you shall afflict your souls, and offer an offering made by fire to the Lord. You shall do no manner of work; *it shall be* a statute forever throughout your generations in all your dwellings. ~ Leviticus 23:27,31 (Day of Atonement)

Speak to the children of Israel, saying: 'The fifteenth day of this seventh month *shall be* the Feast of Tabernacles *for* seven days to the Lord. You shall keep it as a feast to the Lord for seven days in the year. *It shall be* a statute forever in your generations. You shall celebrate it in the seventh month. ~ Leviticus 23:34,41 (Feast of Tabernacles)

Ordinances

Ordinances are specific acts of worship performed as a *memorial.* Scripture specifically says that ordinances are blotted out, so Holy Days that are ordinances, such as the Feast of Unleavened Bread and Blowing of Trumpets, are not expected to be kept. Now there is a slight twist...

The Passover is an ordinance in the Old Testament so it is blotted out. However, Yeshua specifically waited for the Passover to end to have a new Passover with His disciples and this was to reinstitute a new ordinance (Matthew 26:17-19,26-28). The new Passover is to remember how the blood of the lamb (Yeshua) protects us from God's judgment, instead of remembering the blood of the lamb on the doorposts in Egypt.

#55 – Celebrating Salvation

Having abolished in His flesh the enmity, *that is*, the law of commandments *contained* in ordinances, so as to create in Himself one new man *from* the two, *thus* making peace. ~ Ephesians 2:15

Blotting out the handwriting of ordinances that was against us, which was contrary to us, and took it out of the way, nailing it to his cross. ~ Colossians 2:14

Now on the first *day of the Feast* of the Unleavened Bread the disciples came to Jesus, saying to Him, "Where do You want us to prepare for You to eat the Passover?" And He said, "Go into the city to a certain man, and say to him, 'The Teacher says, "My time is at hand; I will keep the Passover at your house with My disciples." ' "So the disciples did as Jesus had directed them; and they prepared the Passover.

And as they were eating, Jesus took bread, blessed and broke *it*, and gave *it* to the disciples and said, "Take, eat; this is My body." Then He took the cup, and gave thanks, and gave *it* to them, saying, "Drink from it, all of you. For this is My blood of the new covenant, which is shed for many for the remission of sins. ~ Matthew 26:17-19,26-28

Speak to the children of Israel, saying: 'In the seventh month, on the first day of the month, you shall have a sabbath-rest, a memorial of blowing of trumpets, a holy convocation. ~ Leviticus 23:24 (Blowing of Trumpets)

You shall eat no leavened bread with it; seven days you shall eat unleavened bread with it, *that is*, the bread of affliction (for you came out of the land of Egypt in haste), that you may remember the day in which you came out of the land of Egypt all the days of your life. ~ Deuteronomy 16:3 (Feast of Unleavened Bread)

About the Author

Sheena Crawford is a writer after God's own heart. She writes blogs, books, and music. She is the author of the What God Told Me book series which focus on God's truth and teaching and encouraging others. Her music consists of poetical lyrics, infused with her love for God, and is typically paired with contemporary instrumentals. She was inspired to write this book at a time when she was raising her son as a single parent. She wanted to teach him how to be a godly man according to Scripture and realized many boys, men, and gentlemen could be blessed by it.